Polly and the Birth Day

D.H. ANDERSON
Illustrations by **STEVEN LESTER**

Lady Thistle, the Horse
BOOK ONE

Polly and the Birth Day

Copyright © 2022 by Donna Anderson Horbal

All rights reserved. No part of this book may be used or reproduced by any means, graphic, electronic or mechanical, including photocopying, recording, taping or by any information storage retrieval system, without the written permission of the author, except in the case of brief quotations embodied in reviews.

Paperback ISBN -978-1-945169-93-9
HardBack ISBN 978-1-945169-94-6
eBOOK ISBN 978-1-945169-95-3

Published by
Little Blessing Books
an imprint of
Orison Publishers, Inc.
PO Box 188, Grantham, PA 17027
www.OrisonPublishers.com

Acknowledgments

Contributing Artist: A. Newman
Contributing Veterinarian: Apryle Horbal, VMD

Meet Lady Thistle

A young horse, whose lively spirit inspired the writing of her real life story. Through her distinctive personality and her talent for connecting with her family and friends, she provided the emotional and illustrative components for this book series.

Waterdam Farm is a peaceful, country spot with happy horses, a playful dog, curious cats, and farmhands who help the family raise and care for horses.

But soon, something very exciting is going to happen…

and it will change Waterdam Farm forever!

Everyone is waiting and watching:
    the horses,
        the farm animal friends,
            and the family.

Because…
 just a few months ago, Polly arrived at the farm!

Polly was a winning racehorse.

After a few years of working and racing, Polly's owners decided it was time for her to retire at Waterdam Farm to become a MOM!

She arrived one crisp, cool evening in February, and as she walked off the trailer, she realized she was at a new and very exciting place.

She heard nickers and whinnies coming from the barn. She saw the beautiful, green, inviting pastures.

Polly looked different from the other horses. She was VERY ROUND and a bit SLOW because there was a little foal growing inside her, getting ready to be born.

The farmhands had prepared a stall for her. They lined it with soft bedding and fresh hay, and they hung buckets of cool water from the walls.

Apryle (pronounced *April*) led Polly to the cozy, little, red barn and offered her treats to settle her nerves. But Apryle quickly realized that Polly only liked apples!

As Polly entered her new home, the other horses greeted her with gentle nods of their heads and nickers, as if to say, "Hello." They made Polly feel welcome!

There was a pile of fresh hay for her in the aisle, too, so she could share her hay time with the others.

Since then, Polly has made many friends at her new home:

Light

Yanik

Mister

Salem

Freeway

and Apryle.

They all know Polly and
love her
VERY MUCH!

Polly settles easily into her new home. She goes out to her field each morning with her new best friend, Daphne.

As they approach the pasture, their mouths water—they can hardly wait to taste the sweet, green, spring grass.

Polly often lies down in the soft pasture. She needs to rest to be ready to give birth to her foal.

At the end of the day, the other horses walk excitedly back to the barn to eat their evening grain. They love to eat their grain!

But Polly walks slowly back for the night because she is very tired.

Polly is surprised and happy to learn that Apryle, one of her new family members, is also her veterinarian!

Dr. Apryle checks Polly and the unborn foal each day. She listens for the baby's heartbeat. She is gentle, and her voice is reassuring.

Dr. Apryle is able to do the daily examination very easily because Polly is a good patient. She seems to know that Dr. Apryle wants to help her.

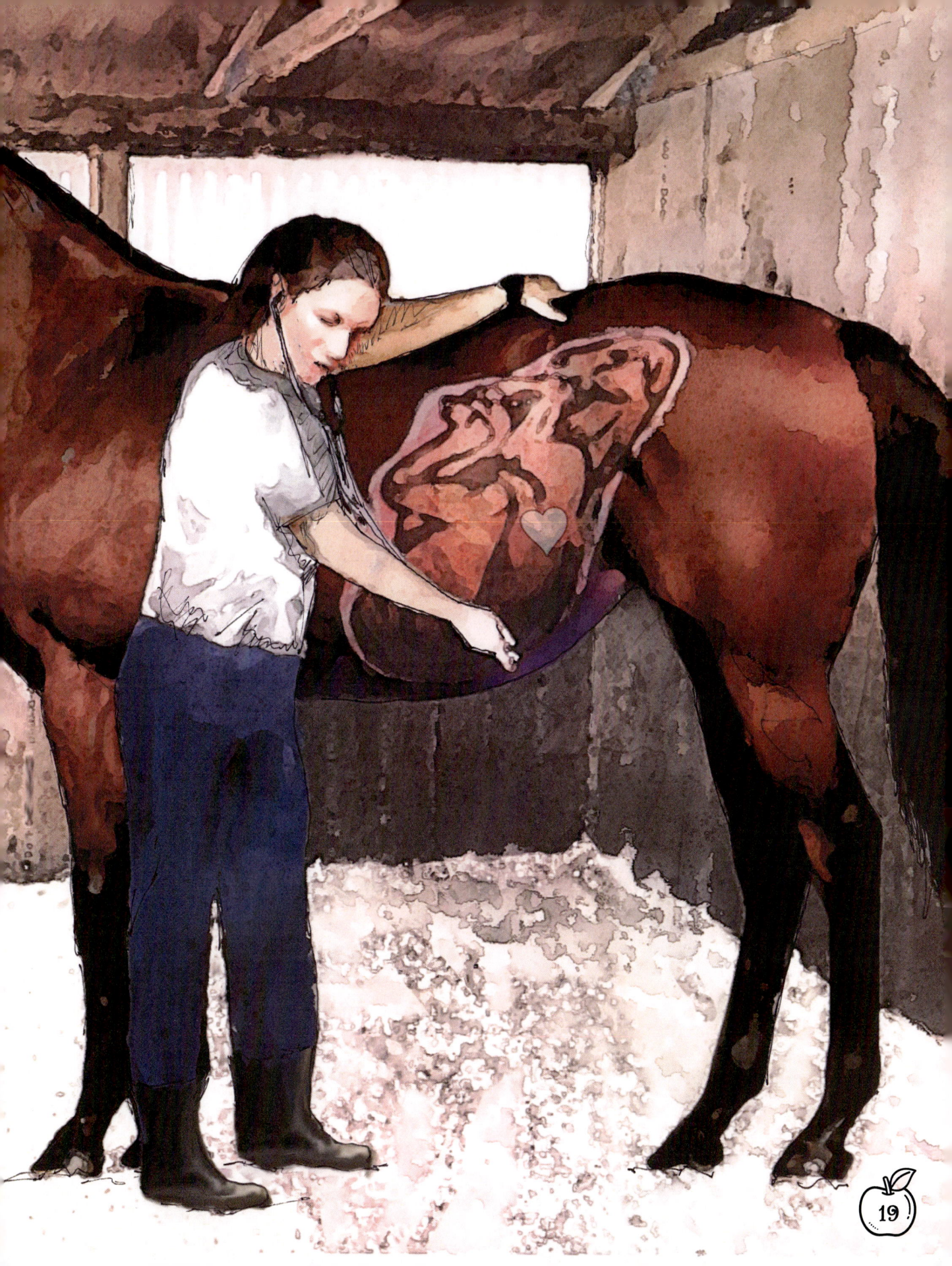

Dr. Apryle tells everyone that when the time comes, Polly will lie down in her stall. So, the family installs a video camera in the rafters of Polly's stall to keep an eye on her. At night, the family and Dr. Apryle watch the camera's livestream on their phones for any sign that Polly is ready to give birth.

Apryle is so excited she cannot put down her phone!

Night after night, nothing happens…
but the horses NEVER forget about eating their hay!

One mid-April night, there is a cool, spring breeze. The sky is especially clear. It is full of bright, sparkling stars and a brilliant, full moon.

Something special is in the air…

On this night, the camera shows that Polly has finally lain down in her stall! The family rushes to her side and calls Dr. Apryle, who is already on her way.

The other horses nicker and snort gently to Polly as they anxiously wait. Everyone hopes the mom and baby will have an easy time.

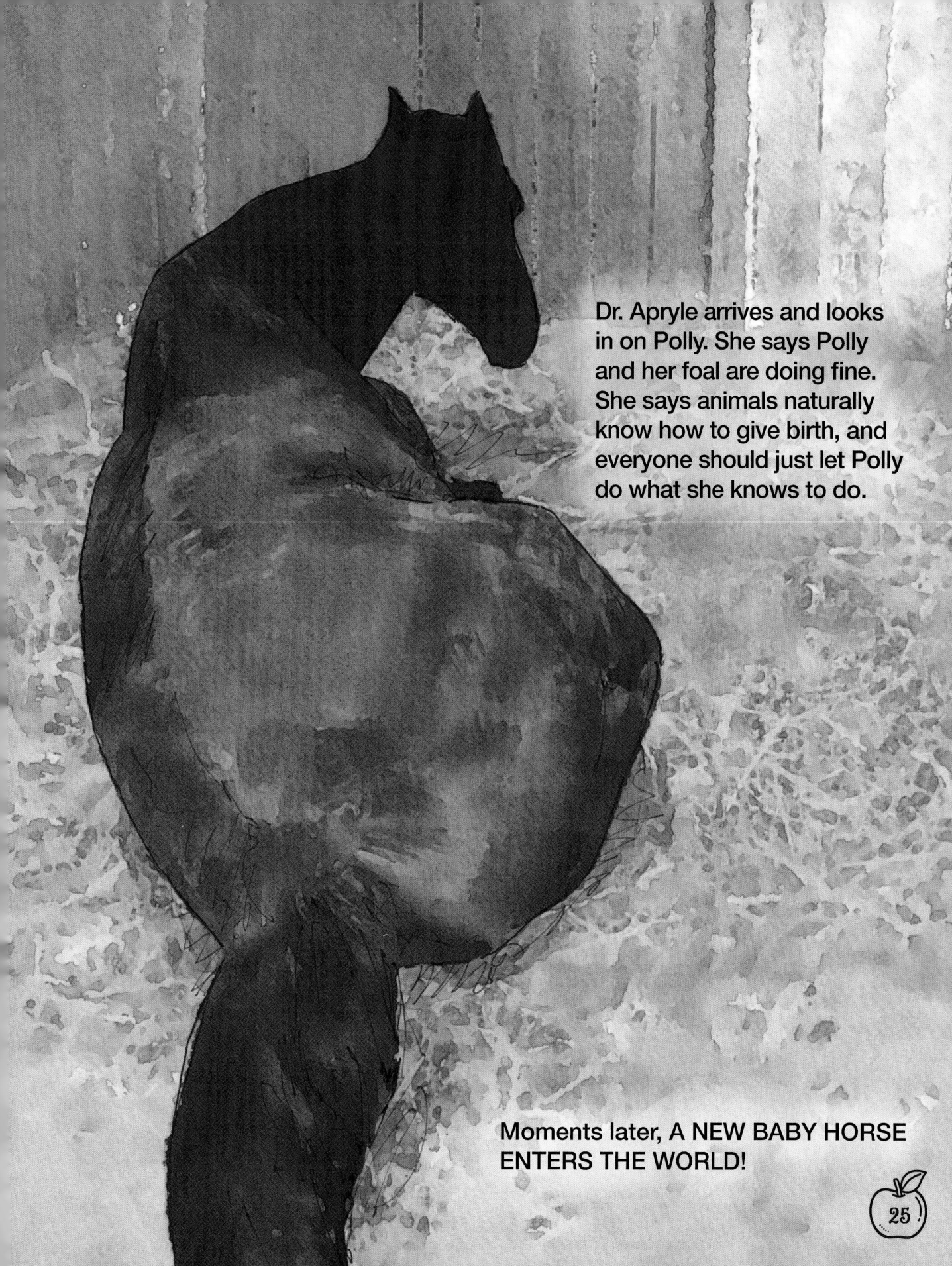

Dr. Apryle arrives and looks in on Polly. She says Polly and her foal are doing fine. She says animals naturally know how to give birth, and everyone should just let Polly do what she knows to do.

Moments later, A NEW BABY HORSE ENTERS THE WORLD!

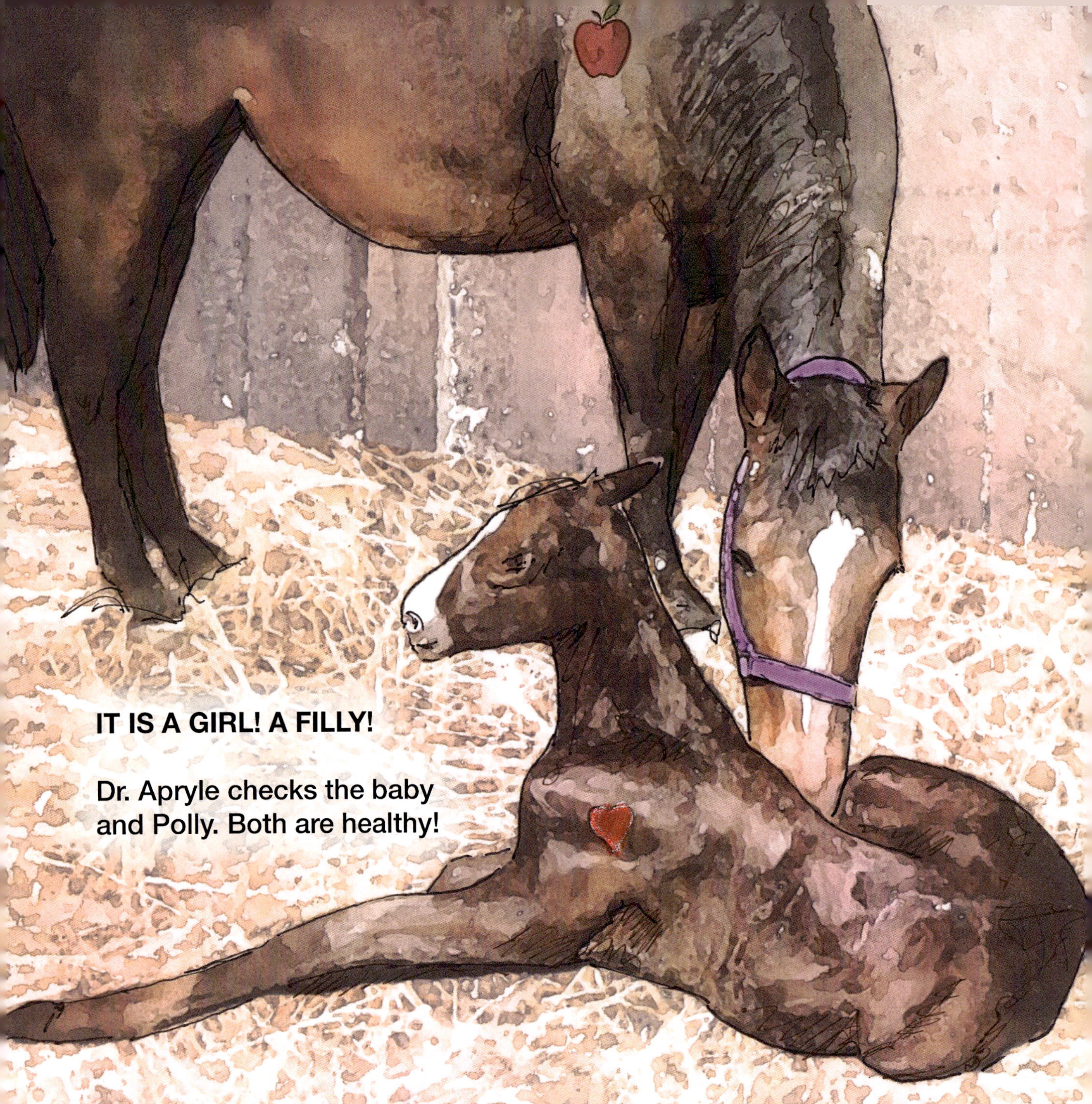

IT IS A GIRL! A FILLY!

Dr. Apryle checks the baby and Polly. Both are healthy!

What an exciting night it is in the barn at Waterdam Farm! Polly is a MOM!

Polly lovingly gazes down at her new baby girl.
The other horses are curious to see the baby. They stretch their necks to get a look, but this will have to wait, because the walls of Polly's stall hide the foal from view. So, they go back to eating their hay.

The family decides her name will be "Lady Thistle." *Lady* seems fitting because her father's name starts with *Lord.* And *Thistle,* because this newborn right away seems spirited—she's already trying to figure out the world around her.

Will she become a winning racehorse like her mother? Or a show horse like her father? What does her future hold?

Lady Thistle

Lady Thistle is now a part of Waterdam Farm, where adventures await her!

Did You Know...?

The *thistle* is the national flower of Scotland, and Dr. Apryle studied surgery on horses in Scotland just before Lady Thistle was born.

Lady Thistle is a Thoroughbred horse. Thoroughbred horses are bred for speed and grace and often are used in races, dressage riding, jumping, and *eventing* (a competition of riding through many types of terrain). But they can be used for other jobs, too!

Her *sire* (father) is Lord Shanakill, and he is from Ireland. Her *dam* (mother) is Precocious Polly, from the United States.

The scientific term used for horses and related animals (like donkeys, mules, and zebras) is *equid* or *equine*.

Horses develop in their mother's *womb* (part of the abdomen) for about eleven months. But sometimes it can take much longer for a *foal to develop* (be ready to be born)—even more than a year.

When the foal is ready to be born, the mother can decide when and where to give birth. She also can pause when giving birth to make sure her surroundings are quiet and calm and few people are around.

Human caregivers need to closely watch their horses to make sure they can help if problems arise when the foal is being born.

You will know a foal is about to be born when milk appears in the mother's udder and dried milk (*wax*) forms on the outside of the udder. This means the foal will be able to eat as soon as it is born.

A vet should check the mother a week or two before the foal is expected to make sure it is positioned to come out headfirst. If it is turned around, a vet or experienced helper should be on hand, as the foal may need help when birth begins. Foals usually *dive* out of the mother, front feet and head first, in the *sac* that protected them and provided them with nutrients and oxygen when they were inside the mother. The *sac* usually breaks open on its own, and the **umbilical cord** connecting the foal to the mother also breaks on its own.

A special part called the **placenta, which** helps to nourish the unborn foal, also passes right after the foal is born. A caregiver needs to check that the whole placenta has come out; if not, the vet must treat the mother right away.

Horses are *prey* animals, which means that in the wild, other animals hunt them. So, horses have developed over time to give birth very fast, usually in an hour or less. Foals stand within an hour of birth and can walk and run during their first day. Nature allowed these traits to develop so horses can escape from *predators* when they live in the wild.

A vet or experienced caregiver needs to be available to help if the birth is taking any longer than one hour in our *domesticated* (companion) horses.

Coming Soon!

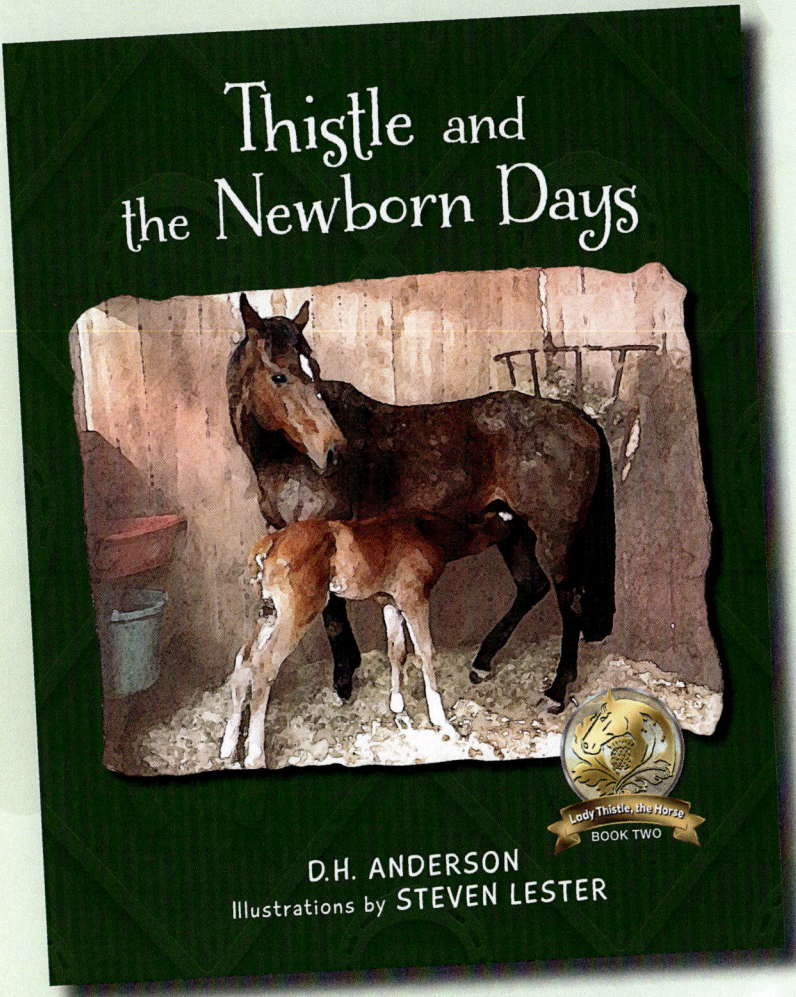

Watch for the Next Book in the Series

Read more stories as young Thistle grows.